PESSIMISM IS FOR LIGHTWEIGHTS

SALENA GODDEN

CW01668771

First published in 2023
by Rough Trade Books

First Edition

ISBN 978-1-914236-22-8

Design by Craig Oldham, Dionne Pajarillaga
Printed in England

All rights reserved. No part of this publication may be reproduced, stored in a retrieval system, copied or transmitted in any form or by any means – electronically, photocopy, recording or otherwise without the permission of the copyright owners.
©Salena Godden, 2023.

The right of Salena Godden to be identified as author of this work has been asserted in accordance with Sections 77 of the Copyright, Designs and Patents Act 1988.

roughtradebooks.com

Pessimism is for Lightweights

30 Pieces of Courage and Resistance

Salena Godden

DEDICATION

This book is dedicated to every person who is using their muscle, their voice, their platform, their work, their art, their time and energy to speak out and stand up for human rights and a better tomorrow. Here are 30 pieces of courage and resistance. Some of these pieces were published in the original pamphlet of '13 pieces of courage and resistance' in 2018. Some pieces I have revised and changed as times are changing and the world is changing. Some of these poems have developed as they were shared and performed at festivals and events. Some of these poems are new and unpublished, some were written as we entered the 2020s and a global pandemic, escalating wars and divisions that would test even the most optimistic and heavyweight among us. Some pieces were inspired by peaceful protest, poems written for people on the front line, pushing for equality, for justice, for peace and freedom. Anti-hate poems. Poems dedicated to people trying to save the NHS. People fighting to save libraries and pubs, the heart of our community and our humanity. People fighting to save the planet. People fighting for justice. This work contains a conversation with the spirit of Hope herself. I thank you, and as always, share these poems with love and solidarity.

Salena Godden

FOREWORD

The phrase 'pessimism is for lightweights' emerged in the dark days of the mid-Trump era, on 5th May 2017. It arrived as I wrote an email to my friend James Burt. The full sentence was, 'Pessimism is easier, of course, but pessimism is for lightweights.'

Back then, the world seemed almost impossibly bleak, as per usual. There was light as well as dark, but you would not have known this from the media you consumed. Green energy became cheaper than fossil fuels years earlier than even the most optimistic predictions, to give one important example, which meant that it now cost more to destroy the climate than it did to repair it. This was a profoundly important moment, but it was not one that the algorithms of social media or the business models of traditional media brought to anyone's attention. They just kept our eyes glued miserably on Trump and Brexit.

I recall feeling let down at the time by a few writers and thinkers I had previously looked up to and seen as wise elders—people I had learnt much from in the past. They shrugged and proclaimed that everything was fucked, and that we were all doomed, and that was all there was to it.

This was a seductive position to adopt, I knew that. You could almost feel a sense of relief when they made it—there was now nothing to be done, so they could relax and do nothing. Once they had adopted this worldview, they had an almost desperate need to protect it and anger would flare up when it was threatened. I felt that if I had shown them a chessboard and asked them to describe it, then they would have looked away and told me I was holding a black square. It was a very strange time. To deny the dark, and to bury your head in the sand and refuse to acknowledge injustice, is generally accepted to be wrong, so I couldn't understand why acknowledging the existence of light had now become taboo. To give up is a luxury. To give up requires the knowledge that the darkness probably won't affect you or your daily life too badly, because if it did you'd fight like hell. To give up, then, is the privilege of abandoning others to their fate. It is to wash your hands of your neighbours, and of the coming generation. When I talk here about giving up, of course, I am not talking about having bad days. We all have those. We are all allowed those. To be knocked down on occasion is different to intentionally dropping to the floor.

On a cold-headed, rational level, optimism is a better strategy than pessimism because an optimist will imagine all sorts of solutions to problems when a pessimist will see no point in trying. Here we're not talking about blind optimism—where you ignore reality and tell yourself that everything will be fine. We are talking about pragmatic optimism. This is where the problem is faced and fully comprehended, and an optimistic outlook is adopted as the best way to deal with it. It is the pragmatic nature of choosing optimism that makes hope so powerful and radical.

I still love the phrase 'pessimism is for lightweights'. It is a warrior's phrase, yet it is somehow both spikey and fluffy. I like the journey it has been on over the last five years, and I like wondering about where it will go from here. A culture with a phrase like that in it doesn't seem quite as hopeless to me as the culture of the mid-Trump years in which it was born. We writers like to kid ourselves that we own the words we produce, and we're very grateful for the copyright laws that keep up this pretence, but deep down we know that it isn't true. Words live in as many heads as they can, and their point of origin is irrelevant.

It is the vibrancy and the potential that they offer their hosts that matters.

Words shape ideas, which shape attitudes, which shape actions. Thank you for carrying these particular words forward.

John Higgs
Brighton, August 2022

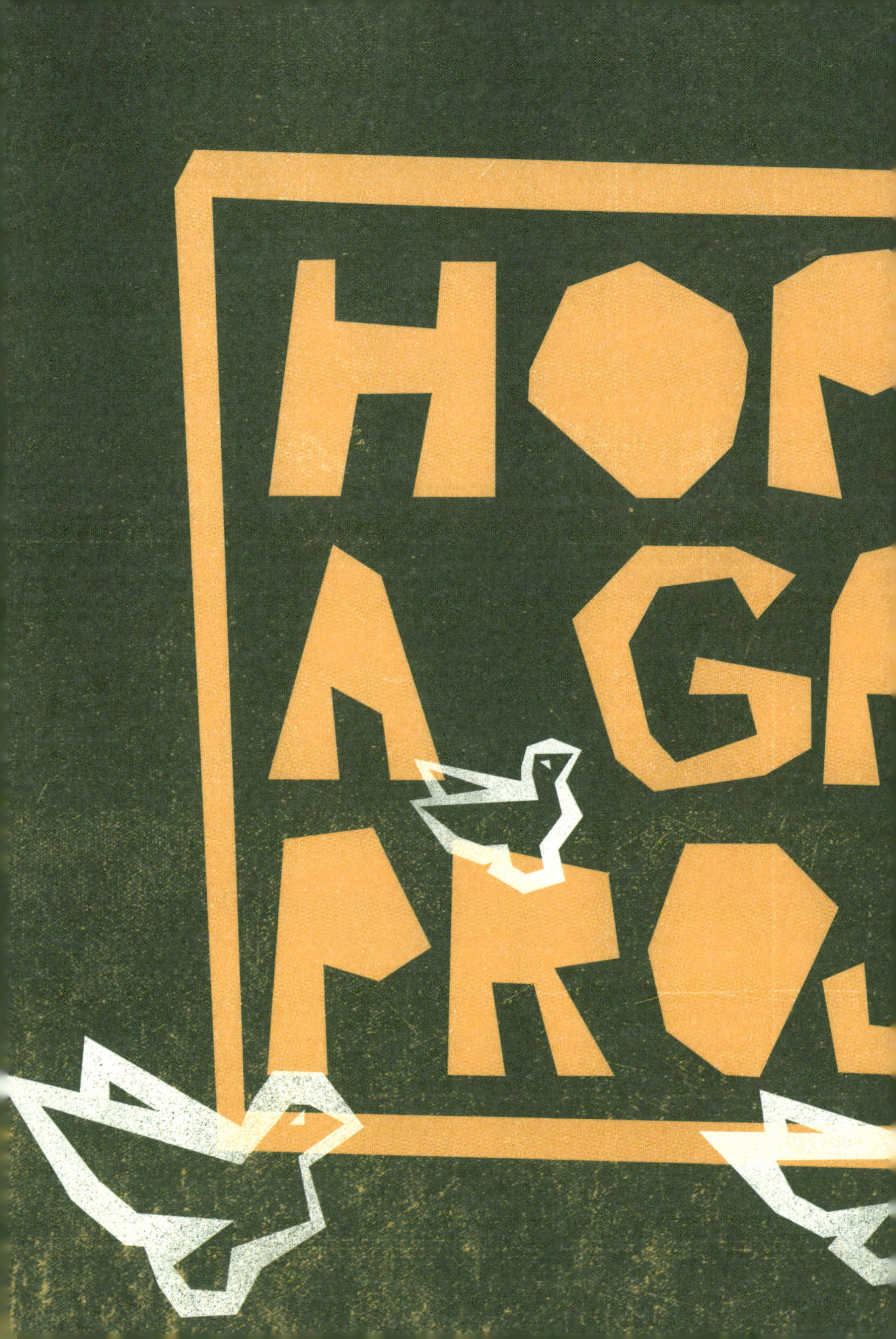

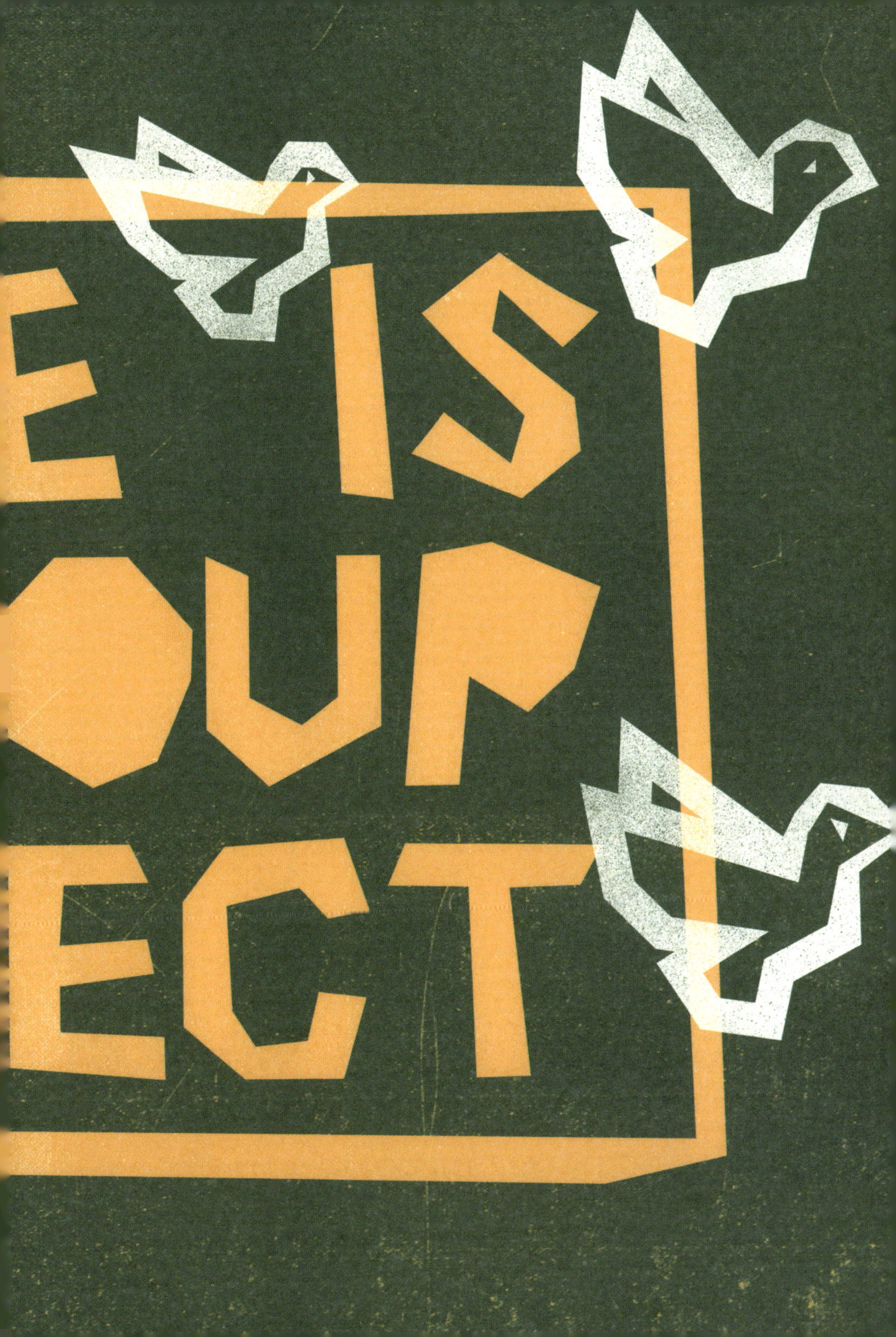
E IS
OUP
ECT

Welcome to Hope

Here's your map, she says
This is where you always are
See here, the mountains of vivid life
Make a boat of books, read them all
Sail down this mighty dream river
Through forests of wonder
Look how the trees grow ever good
How the sky holds its own
Nature is so loud in her gardening
Your soul is your compass
Kindness isn't at the border
Caring is not the city
But change is in the wind
And wild is the weather
Home is a feeling
And now is where we are
She nudges me awake
Welcome to Hope
She sings, welcome to Hope
Get up! Get up! Get up!
Hope is here and love knows
We have so much to do.

Pink Moon

the night is still / as April's pink moon rises / lying / in his hot and fevered bed / the billionaire will meet an angel / walking in the soft shoes of a nurse / moonlight washes the city / as the hungry cry and shiver / the Thames shimmers / in the shadow of Westminster / as he watches / the nurse pours water / how can he be so blind to miracles / how the angel is the nurse / the hospital is a cathedral / how everything is nothing / and money is nowhere / and your love is here / and your heart is now / and life is a debt / you pay back in kind / and your soul / like a wide hungry mouth / screaming / feed me the truth / the first lesson / a disaster teaches us / is how fragile this is / blood and air / water and bone / with the same / super moon / super moon / with the same / water and bone / blood and air / is how fragile this is / a disaster teaches us / the first lesson / feed me the truth / screaming / like a wide hungry mouth / and your soul / you pay back in kind / and life is a debt / and your heart is now / and your love is here / and money is nowhere / how nothing is everything / the hospital is a cathedral / how the angel is the nurse / how can he be so blind to miracles / the nurse pours water / as he watches / in the shadow of Westminster / the Thames shimmers / as the hungry cry and shiver / moonlight washes the city / walking in the soft shoes of a nurse / the billionaire will meet an angel / in his hot and fevered bed / lying / as April's pink moon rises / the night is still.

Soup

Imagine if seven people from seven nationalities
Came to your home to share one pot of soup,
You would have seven conflicting versions of that soup.

One would write to note the flavour. Another the heat.
Someone would write about the meaning of soup.
The size of the portions.
The memory the soup triggers.
Too salty.
Not enough meat.
This is a stew?
It's more a casserole!
This soup is a meal in itself!
I'm gluten intolerant!

The hungriest person at the table might just write—Thank you

This is human nature—
We look around the table and
Examine the world as we do these dinner guests.
We note our differences—
Skin and manners and clothes and language.
And we forget to sing!

We forget to celebrate that we are one,
That the act of love was sitting down together
And sharing the pot of soup in the first place.

And we say nothing
As they put someone in prison
For using a fork to eat their soup.

We silence the person that slurps soup from the bowl.

We ignore all women because...
Well, what does a woman know about soup anyway?

Some around the table demand bread with their soup,
Others feel entitled to the whole pot of soup, just for them.
There's one, there is always one, who will spit in the soup
So that the soup is ruined for everyone,
And sadly this is all human nature too.

I am too sad to finish this poem about soup
I'll just say I have so much to be grateful for
I'm so lucky I have a warm kitchen
I have a pot and some vegetables

Today
I'm gonna make time
Today
I'm gonna make love
Today
I'm gonna make soup

Fuck war
Make soup

Courage is a Muscle

Courage is the muscle
we use when we speak,
if we're being talked over
and told we're too weak.
And when we get weary
and when it gets tough,
it's our united courage says—
Enough is enough.

Courage is the muscle
we work night and day,
to get equal rights
to get equal pay.
Our blood is taxed
our blood is shame,
our courage unites us
for we all bleed the same.

Courage is the muscle
we flex when we must,
courage is the muscle
for truth and for trust.
Courage is the muscle
we use when we speak,
if we're being walked over
and told we're too weak.

And when we get weary
we march side by side,
1000 years we're still marching
with courage and with pride.

It's All About the Pathways

K said
we make
neural pathways
in our head
for people
to process ideas
we make connections
and repetitions
K said
grief hurts and
losing someone hurts
and death is painful
because your head
is dissolving
the neural pathway
that was made
for that person
it grows in your head
K said
like a branch of ivy
in your head
K said
and it works the other way
for example
a racist has made a
neural pathway
of hate
a pattern of repetition
a narration of a version
of events
and the more
the racist repeats that story
the thicker that branch grows

when we latch
onto an idea
like loving someone
or like
hating someone
we make a pathway
sticking to one narration
one version
about a person or subject
until the ivy knots
in our head
K said
and the branch
gets thicker and thicker
the pathways
we create
love and hate
we get stuck
and we
cannot see
reason or light.

I Saw Goody Proctor Jogging Without a Face Mask

I saw Goody Proctor
and John Proctor
walking side-by-side
holding hands
two-abreast with
Devil's breath

I saw Goody Proctor
clapping for the NHS
she were too very close
to her neighbour
and both
without bra
or manners

I saw Goody Proctor
under the full moon
this very week
she was a-gazing up
with bare
unwashed hands
unshaved legs
and virus eyes

I saw Goody Proctor
and John Proctor
they were not near home
and they were under
the open sky sun
and they had
two whole toilet rolls
each in merriment

I saw Abigail Williams and
Elizabeth Proctor together
and close as demon's breath
with eggy mouths and
unwashed knotted hair
and no lipstick
nor hand sanitizer

I saw Goody Proctor
doing yoga with a black cat
and she did warrior pose
'twas the dance
of the Devil's whore

I saw Goody Proctor
have a double Baileys
with her breakfast coffee
to take the edge off

I saw Goody Proctor
cough once and
cough twice and
then thrice cough
and her flem
was the black of
Satan's cock and
her droplets
made sick all

I saw Goody Nurse
be told she be
unwelcome and
immigrant of
foreign blood

I saw Goody Nurse
unpaid proper
and made to
risk her own life
for nowt but
a hand clapping

The Day We Stopped

There was hardly any resistance. You'd think there would be more panic, more protests, more anger, more about it on the news. They pulled up in plain vans and marched into public spaces—the parks and the shopping centres in broad daylight, they read charges, arrested people, one by one.

I stared, we stared, we all stood still and stared, as people were calmly selected and handcuffed and escorted away.

I was captured, but even I hardly resisted. You'd think that I would make more fuss, that I would be dragged, kicking and screaming. But I seem to recall apologising to them in their uniforms, with their masks and guns.

We were taken away. To a place just like here and now, but we were not free to leave. In the beginning we tried to run away, we plotted and planned how to escape. I remember how we whispered in the dark, we said it was wrong, we wept and said we missed our lives our families, our lovers, our children.

I tried to escape, once, I ran for it, I got as far as a dream, but a hand covered my mouth.

As time passed I grew to become a model prisoner. I learned how to be subservient, obedient and quiet. How strange it was when the singing stopped, that is what I am remembering most. The deafening silence. The whispering stopped, the nudge of notes stopped. Funny how this place was once all bite and scratch and graffiti, but one by one we stopped shouting and kicking and fighting and running away.

This place was inside and there was no outside to run to. This was as normal as home. Our freedom was past, our past erased.

Our history was a burnt book. We were as sedate as bored lions in the zoo. We stopped asking questions and making demands, we ate whatever we were fed and did as we were told. And when it was dark, we slept dreamlessly.

We stopped seeing the walls, because we stopped looking.

But now I am here. I stand in an empty space. Looking up at a still and grey sky. I am alone for the first time in a very long time. I am walking in a park. There's a damp chill in the air. Wet grass, the crunch of dead leaves below my feet. A silence and stillness.

I'm not being followed, or chased or pursued by dogs, but I keep walking because I'm unsure if I have escaped or if I am still dreaming? If I am inside or outside, if I even existed? Can anyone see me? Will anyone read this? I don't know if I am sleepwalking.

I walk around the park perimeter and write this in my head. I keep walking inside the railings in a never-ending circle. I memorise this feeling. I know these tears. It is a sad and strange poem, all of this feels sad and strange. I sing these words, they spiral in my remembering. Over and over again, an ancient song, haunting me, calling to me...

The day we get lost is the day we got lost is the day we stop dreaming is the day we stop longing is the day we stop fighting is the day we think we are free is the day we stop running is the day we stop dreaming is the day we forget is the day we remember is the day we stopped speaking is the day we forget the words is the day we stop reading is the day we stop writing is the day we stop praying and wishing and hoping is the day we stop loving is the day we stop living is the day we lose the colour and the light and the warmth and the joy is the day we get lost is the day we are lost is the day we stop laughing is the day we believe we are free is the day we stop dreaming is the day we stop running is the day we stop fighting is the day we stop singing is the day we stopped singing is the day we stop singing and one by one we fall one by one we fall and one by one we fall

Silent.

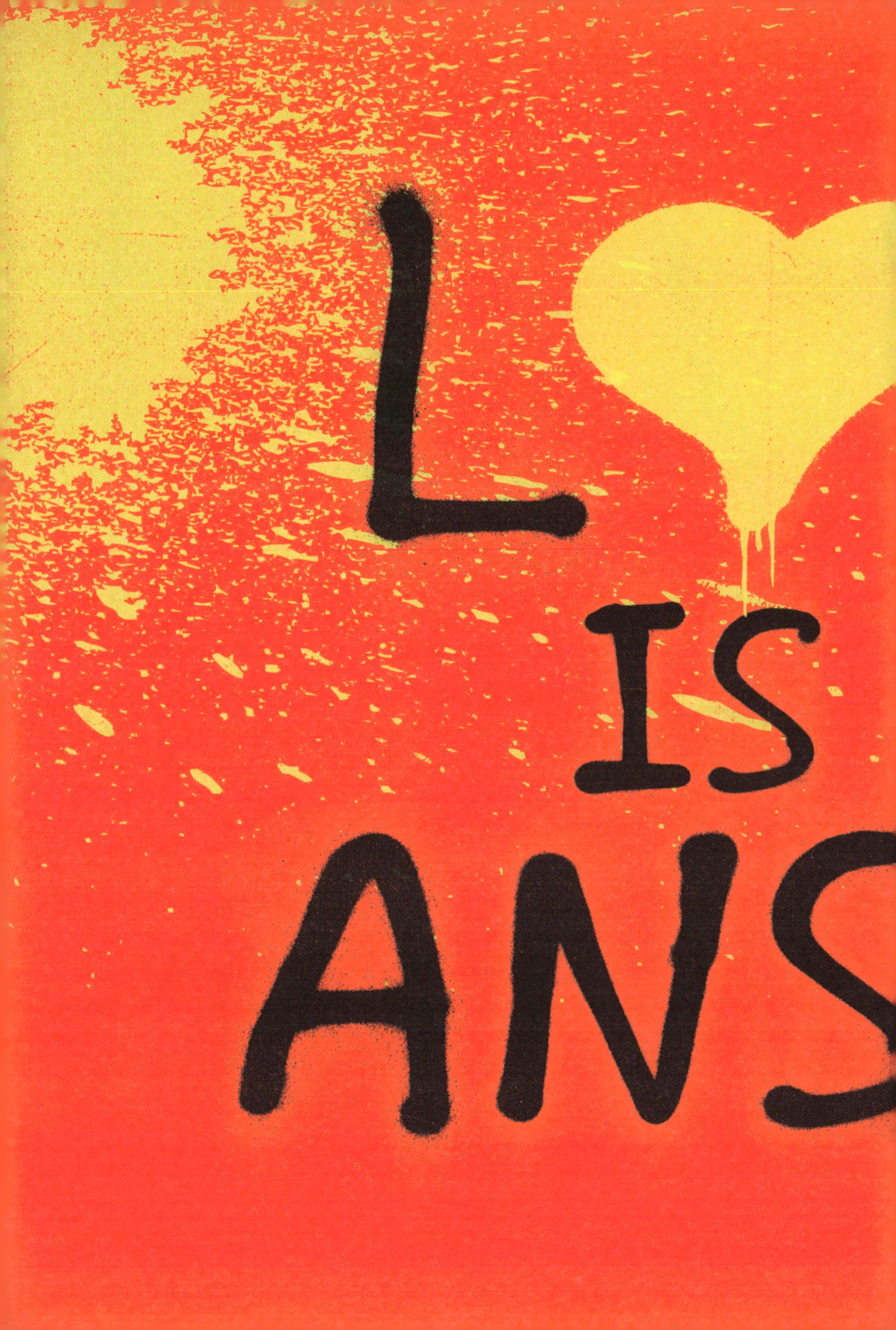
L
IS
ANS

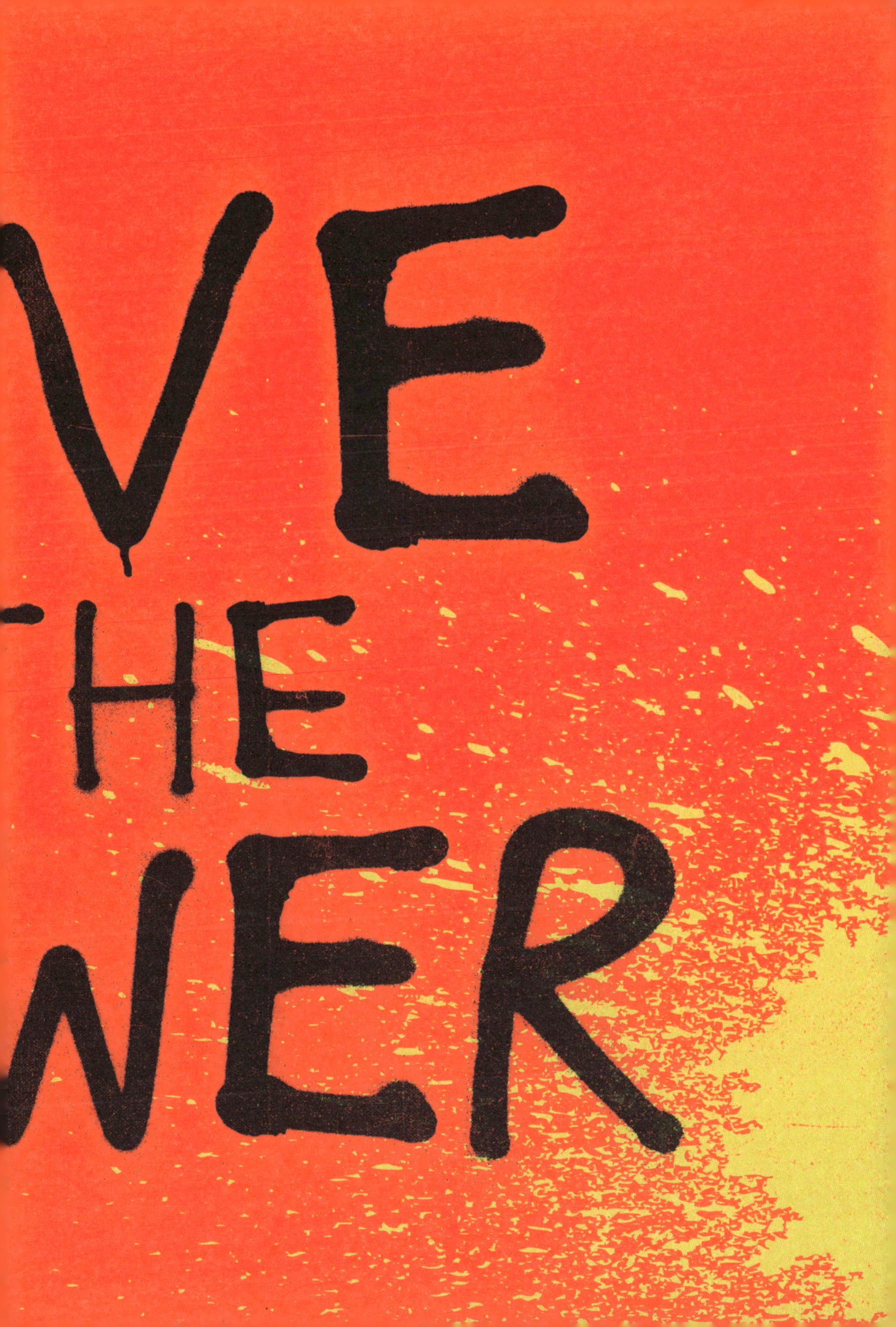
VE
HE
WER

No Holds Barred

We're outside a pub
and she's yelling
telling me to
get back on my boat

My friends say she's just racist
but I put down my rum
and walk over and ask
do you need a hug?

I stand with open arms
as wide as a map of the world
she bursts into tears
I hold her for a while

My jacket gets stained
in orange foundation,
my lapels are streaked
with black mascara

The pub is rumbling
under the mad full moon,
and the spring tide
crashes to shore

My heart is a boat
my ancestor's longships
my grandmother's Windrush
the rubber dinghies sunk without trace.

Not Every Thing is True

and
all your thoughts
are not facts
you dream
a hundred choices
narrate your life
in a hundred voices
which make you
stop and start
but not every thing
you think is true
not every think
you thing is true
some of these ideas
they are no good
they are not
magic gold
but jangled bits of
rusty razor songs
and lies that
you have stored
to cut yourself
again and again
these fakeries
are buried
in dialogues
you keep like
train tickets
to feeling bad
again
to teach yourself
a lesson
to remind

yourself to remember
to think again
another shit thing
again
but not not not
every thing
you think
is true
the truth
was a squeaky
squeeze box
nasty noises
no excuses
just be quiet
just be kind
just be
as kind as
you can be
because not every
thing you think
is real not every
think you think
is real
it's just you
feeling feelings
again
and not every
thing is true
at least be the
best of you
be there
for you
that is the best

you can do
because not every
stinking thinking
dirty shitty thought
you have is real
not every thing
is true
and don't forget
you make stuff up
you do
you really do
and not every
thing is
true

HO

I

ENE

PE

RGY

So, This is How it Starts

so,
this is how
it starts in books
they burn
or ban books
in books
that imagine
a world
that burns
or bans books
it starts there
with books that dare
to say this is how it is
or this is how it was
or this is how it could be
and if you
read books
you will know
from books
that this is
how it ends
so, this is how
it starts

Point Nemo

When I get home
I hang my snowy clothes
on the radiator
I make tea and sit
at my laptop and search maps
I am seeking peace.
I type in: P E A C E
the internet takes me to
the holiest places on earth
I scroll images of Bangladesh, Ethiopia and Malawi
they look too busy to me
too many people, too many faces
I search again for peace: P E A C E
a website shows me a top ten
of the most peaceful countries:
I see a shepherd in New Zealand
a postman in Iceland
a fisherman in Finland
my fingertips type again:
P E A C E
I search to find the most remote places
Barrow in Alaska and
Chang Tang in Tibet
I search for peace on earth:
P E A C E
where is peace?
where is the peace?
where is the most peaceful place?
PEACE. PEACE. PEACE
I noisily tap the word into my laptop
PEACE. PEACE. PEACE
I find the most remote place on earth
Point Nemo

it is in the South Pacific Ocean
I gaze at it: Point Nemo
I stare for a very long time
it is one thousand, four hundred miles
from anything and from anyone
there is nothing but
open sky and open water
open seas and open air
it is nowhere
and it is everywhere
this must be it
the centre of peace
P E A C E
I look at it
yes this is the place
a floating island
of plastic and ropes and
dead turtles and shit
and deep down
below the surface
a graveyard of
fallen spacecraft debris
and junk and crap
I shut my laptop
snow drifts past my window
a deep lapis-blue dusk light
I take a deep breath and exhale
I watch my breath fog up the windowpane
I write SOS
where is PEACE
where is the peace
inside there
outside here

Chapter

I long to skip
to the next chapter,
where the kings panic
and turn on each other,

a mirror smashes
to reveal it is
all an illusion

the lie eats
its young,
and destroys
itself,

the kings
are no more—
they were
sabotaged
by their own
cowardice
and greed,

a cloud passes
a new light
washes
all grief away,
a soft rain
on a new dawn,

we hear
bird song,
our children rise
and play,

the people
exhale,
in one big
easy breath,

we recover
we heal and
plant seeds,
we choose love
we live in
peace.

Gentle Reminder

The nurse isn't fussed
if you haven't had a trim,
she's looking at your cervix
not your lovely hairy quim.

The nurse don't care
if it's jungle or fluff,
it's about saving lives
not a nice neat muff.

So I don't know why I did it?
I panicked and it's weird,
got myself in a lather
and removed my lady beard.

Over trimming, over thinking
and worrying about the 'sitch,
when my bush grows back
it's gonna really itch.

But the nurse don't care
if you haven't had a shave,
she's looking at your cervix
and more lives to save.

Insert

here a poem
in response
to the
{...}
I could
write a new
piece
about the
{...}
but the
{...}
were total
{...}
last week
and the week
before that
it is
relentless
the
{...}
are
constant
{...}
shameless
{...}
and they
will be
{...}
next week
and the week
after that
because
they're total

and utter
{...}
please
feel free
to read
any of
my previous
poems
about the
{...}
grimacing
on the
front page
every morning
like
{...}
apologies
in advance
to everyone
except you
{...}
you total
{...}

Sorry to Trouble You

they will call them
the troubled poets
I love poets
I love poets
causing trouble
and troubling
other poets
poets troubled
by drunkenness
and nightmares
and insomnia
troubled poets
troubled by depression
heart sick isolation
I love troubled poets
troubled by
poverty and hunger
writing poetry
by a tea light with
a stolen job centre pen
a spider for an audience
a cigarette for heat
drinking cooking lager
I love troubled poets
troubled by conflict
scribbling poems
in an immigration centre
on their own wrist
with a piece of glass
I love troubled poets
troubled in refugee camps
troubled in children's homes
troubled in shop doorways

sleeping rough
in rain-soaked rags
relying on food banks
eating cold beans from the tin
using newspaper for a sanitary towel
troubled poets
troubled in the trenches
troubled by abuse and torture
poets writing poems in blood
and given public lashings
for writing
just for writing blogs
and publishing poems
poets stoned to death
in the town square
for their trouble
troubled poets
writing and fighting
for human rights
troubling themselves
with all that is unsaid
and all that is meant
inside the graffiti
I love a poet's
troubled cry
thank fuck
for every poet
bless you
we salute you
troubled poets
troubled
by silence
violence

troubled by
lack of light
lack of truth
troubled by the
troubles of the world
rocks in your pockets
stones under the tongue
wading into icy water
tying a hangman's noose
around a troubled throat
gargling your
troubled words
to the end
I love troubled poets
that trouble themselves
peeling onions
in a Calais kitchen
protesting
at Downing Street
remember when Stormzy sang—
You think we forgot about Grenfell?
I loved that
I love troubled poets
troubled poets
sharing, airing
their troubles
in public
poets who
trouble themselves
with trouble
I love the poets
who are bothering
to trouble us

poets who bother
to trouble themselves
troubled poets
who are troubled
by all of this
this terrible
terribly troubling
troubled, troubled world

Who is Us, Who is Them

after war

who cleans up
who sweeps streets
who heals wounds

after war

who mends roads
who teaches school
who builds hospitals

after war

who plants seeds
who makes soup
who holds grief

after war

who is broken
who is lost
who is we

who is hope
who is love
who is peace

after war

Ortolan

treat your
new ideas
like ortolan,
tiny songbirds,
lock them
in a box and
gorge them
on figs,
drown them
in Armagnac,
then roast
them and
eat them
whole,
small bones
and all,
put a cloth
over your head
as you feast
and inhale
the fumes.

Red

You should see what I made red
You should see what I made red
You should see my art

Look at my beetroot chutney
Look at me and my red soupy pants

You should see me now
On all fours groaning
Rocking back and forth
On my haunches
Breathing into it
Breathing out of it
Clinging to my hot water bottle like a life raft
Low frequency cramps
Punctuated by knitting needle cramps
With extra kick and prick
Like a scissors' jab and snip
Inside my bloody hole

And the product is blackcurrant jelly, redcurrant syrup
You should see what I made red
You should see what I made red
You should see my art
The sheets, the sheets, the sheets
I made all the sheets red
All the bed a pool of red heat

In the bath there are floating globs
Chunky bloody marmalade
Black cherry vomit
Farmhouse strawberry jam
I'm having a very heavy time man!
But I won't make too much of a fuss
Just leave me here to bleed to death
The last thing we want is any fuss
Just leave me here to drown in my own blood

You should see what I make red
You should see what I made red
Real red and vivid as black cherry juice
Kidneys in my frying pants
My pyjamas are my butcher's apron

So, I used a whole packet of pads in one day!
Remarkable! Come on! Give me a round of applause!
I wanted to go into my local pub
Throw the empty packet down on the bar and yell—

Hey everyone,
I am having the biggest one!
I used a whole packet in one day!

And then I'd demand free drinks
How the pub will applaud and cheer
And how everyone will slap me on the back for having such a big one

In the movie of this month
my period would be played by Bruce Willis: Bleed Hard

But...
This blood does not come from violence
This blood does not come from murder
This blood is not my death
There are no bullets or knives
This is no wound or sickness
This blood is not a weakness
This blood is my moon
This blood is my time
This blood is my last big fireworks display
This blood is my farewell dance
This blood is all me
And yet this blood disgusts us the most
More than any blood
More than the blood on the hands of man's bloody war
This blood disgusts us most
This shameful blood, this quiet blood
Shush! Don't mention the lady blood
Shush! Don't mention this discreet blue lady blood

Yet we had to pay tax for this silent blood
This blood of ours is so very disgusting—
And yet so taxable
So, come on then,
I'll get my money's worth

Come see, see what I paint red
You should see what I made red
Come see, come see what I made red
You should see my mess
The bathroom, the bedroom
Every towel and white pant
Everything, stained with my stink and tang
The whole world I paint it red, red, red
Come see, come see, come see
You should see what we made red
You should see, come see,
See RED

Anything you can do
We can do bleeding
Anything you can do
We can do bleeding
We can do anything
Flooding with blood

Old Blood and Young Teeth

A life is so short,
When you consider the age
Of the temples and cathedrals,
Built with the faith and old blood of men,
Who lived short lives and then died,
In the name of their Gods
And their Gods' immortality.

Consider the age of that gold Buddha
It is older than the crippled tree
That was planted when it was erected,
But younger than the river beneath it.

And the ocean must be oldest of all,
And the years of the sun and the moon?
Who is eldest? The sun or the moon?
And the age of fire, how old is fire?
How old is water? Is rain older than flame?

And the teeth in your head are so young, my love
The teeth in your head are so young,
The teeth in your head are so young compared to your brain.

What thoughts your brain had before your teeth grew
And your old heart, how faithfully it beats, old timer
Your ears listened and heard you scream
As that first tooth tore through
And the first thing
Your first tooth gnawed
Was your own finger.

All of us had to grow teeth last,
Every one of us had to grow our teeth last,
So smile now, show me your young teeth,
Smile and show us all your spring chicken tooth,
Smile and let your first dream soar,
Smile now and feel that love beat in your old chest,
And shine out of those big old eyes of yours,
Your shiny old eyes in your old bone skull head,
But oldest of all is your old, old blood,
Your blood is as old as time,
And I love you,
And I love every drop.

Sushi

Do you remember the first time a man fed you sushi? It was a long time ago. Do you remember? He took you to the new Japanese restaurant. A bright and gladly lit place where the food goes around on a conveyor belt. Do you remember watching the food going around? Each plate of food assembled on rainbow plates just like the pictures on the wall. Do you remember the first bite? The first taste? The snap of pink ginger. The tuna was red as watermelon, but the texture, it was like his wet red tongue, but cold, raw, fish. Then the hard slap was wasabi, the sting, your nose tingling with blood. Do you remember the first time he hit you? Do you remember the first time you had sushi? The first time you were slapped? Do you remember the shock of the first time you were slapped by a man? Do you? Do you remember the heat? And the sushi? Your hot cheek. Stinging. Do you remember the pop of orange eggs? Do you remember the first time you had sushi? How strange is hot wine though, you said. Hot wine? It's not hot wine, he said. It is sake. Not wine. Sake. So embarrassed. Red cheeks. Do you remember? Do you remember you said sorry? Sorry. You said sorry the first time you were hit by a man. Remember how you apologised and how he cried, and you said sorry again. And he went very quiet and thundery and you felt guilty in his weather. Do you remember the guilt you felt the first time you made a grown man cry for hitting you? He cried. Do you remember making a grown man cry? Do you remember you did that? Remember the first time you saw a man in tears?

How you'd never seen a man cry before, and you didn't know men cried like that, like girls, shaking shoulders, eyes all full up of sad and tears and, plop-plop-plop, tears weaving through his grown man bristles. His rough man cheeks all wet and it was your fault. You made him cry. You did this. He loves you so much. Sorry you said. Your cheek still hot. The inside of your arms bruised from him holding you and shaking you. Shaking you and shaking you like a wet dog. Shaking you blue. Blue bruises. Purple bruises. Green bruises. All colours down the inside of your arms. Bruises in fingerprints. You could see each fingerprint in the bruises where he held you tight and shook you and shook you. And it's your own fault. You're too wilful. You'll lose him if you aren't careful. Because he's ten years older than you, so he knows what real love is. And he paid for dinner and you had sushi and it's posh. And it's raw fish. And you didn't know sushi was raw fish because you're fifteen and he's twenty-five and he knows things about the big wide world. And later he was all drink up, drink fast, eat this and eat that. Your mouth was stuffed full and you swallowed it all up to please him. You swallowed it all down to show him what a big girl you are. Do you remember that sashimi tuna tongue? Do you remember he hit you? Pulled and pushed you? Do you remember the first time a man hit you? The first time. The last time. The first time. The last time. Red. Raw. Sushi. Remember the first time. Remember the last time. Let that be the last time.

Christine

His mother
called me
a good time girl
they all said
I was just looking
for a good time
I was a teenager
I thought looking
for a good time was a good thing
and her son, he was good
he gave me a good time, alright
he called me darling
much later
they all called me
prostitute
forever and ever
how fast they all turned their backs
so quick to betray daughters,
to protect the good old boys.

The Letter

Dear,
I hope you're well
I hope you're warm and dry
A safe place to lie your head
Some oranges, some fresh bread
I hope home is safe and sound
Shelter from a storm and high ground
I hope you make time to read and grow
And water all those seeds you sow
You know, you come, you know, you go
That is how the humans flow
Your geography is at best ambient
Temporary, transient
Clocks are maps, time is past
Nothing isn't meant to last
Fight or flight or run and flea
Not one of we can feel free
If some of we are locked in fear
That's how we've always been, my dear

My dear,
I post this in a letter
I hope you can hold each other better
Wind and fire, fuel and wars
Weary feet cross desert floors
Broken boats and brutal sea and
Human greed and tyranny
Displacement, homeless, rearranging
Constant change is you, growing, changing

So, I'll enclose a breath for healing
A match to burn all ill-feeling
A monarch butterfly wing
your migration is a magnificent thing

Here's some lint for all you built
A peppermint to suck and soothe your guilt
Your burning cities, your barren land
You drown with sharks, you choke on sand
Where do we bandage our world today?
Where's the root of all the pain?
Everything is blood stained
It's buried in your DNA
You carry all your yesterday
Clocks are maps, time is fast
Everything is meant to pass
Fight or flight or run and flee
Not one of we can be free
If some of we are locked in fear
That's how we've always been, my dear

My dear,
I Hope you're well,
I Hope you're warm and dry
A safe place to lie your head
Some oranges, some fresh bread
Clean water and clean air
Space to grow, room to share
Home is just a marble in the sky
I roll it blue and green and I
Hope I am and Hope am I
See all that free sky up above

Live with Hope
Live with love,

With love,
Hope

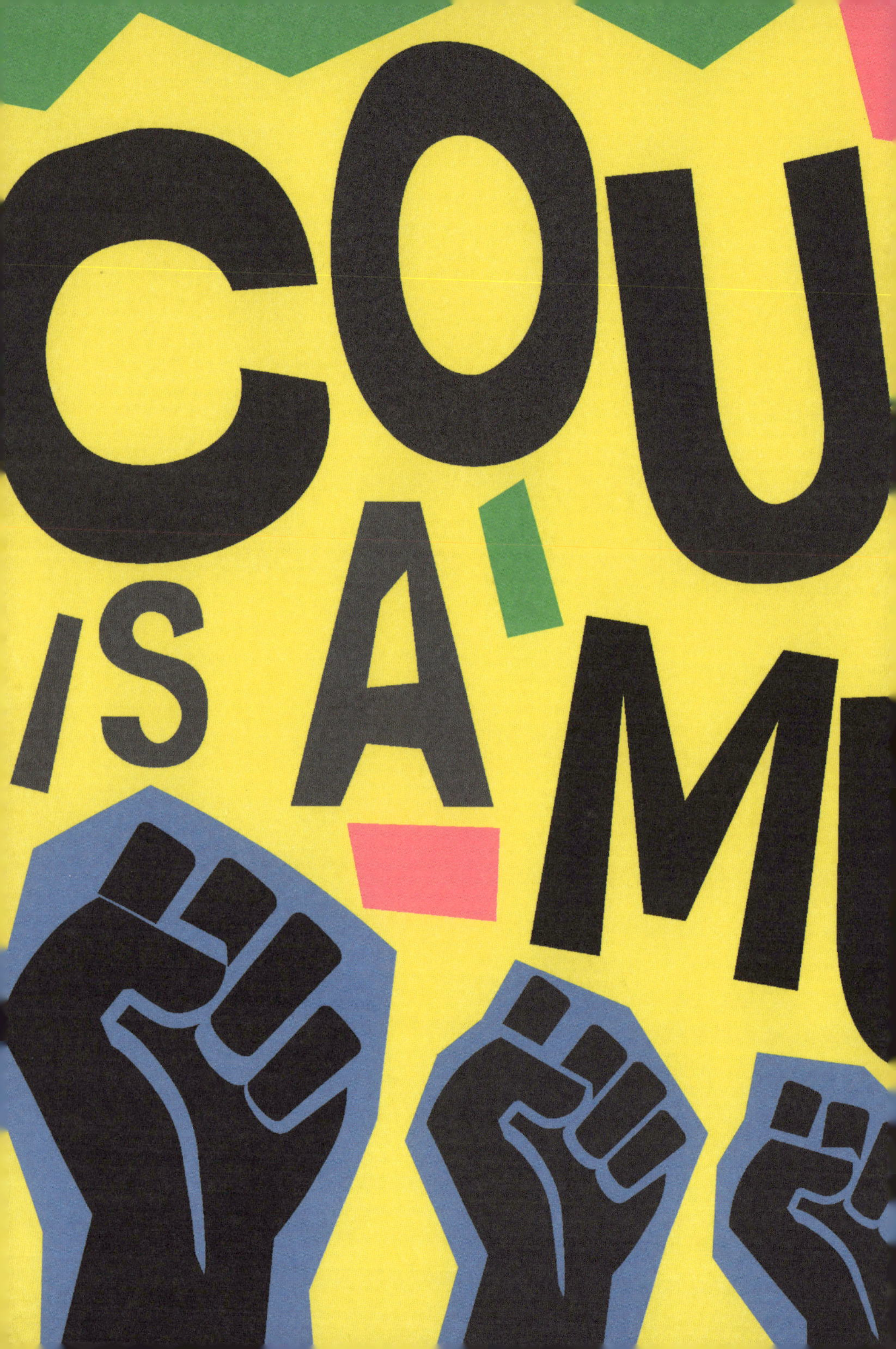
COU
IS A M

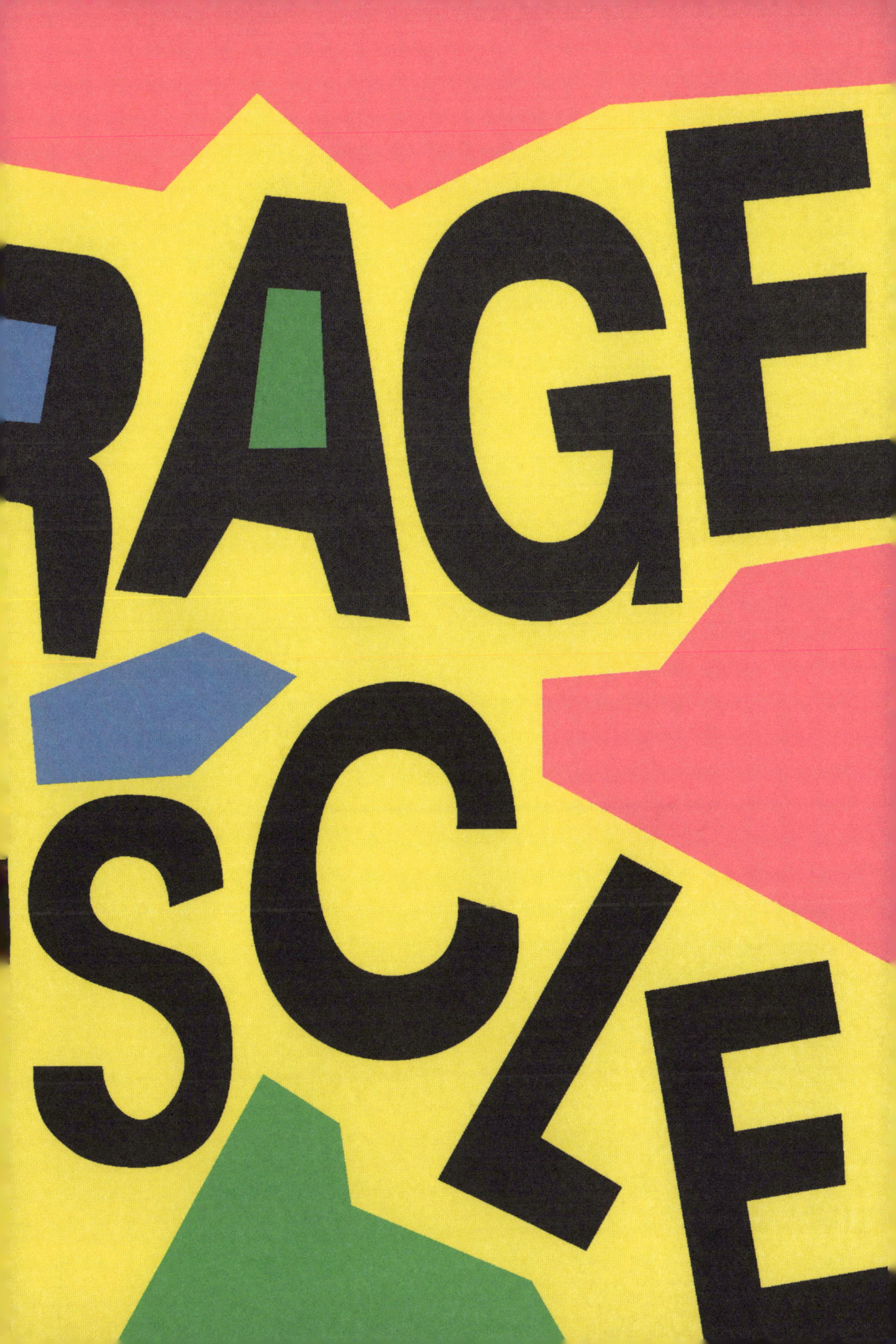
RAGE
SCLE

It Isn't Punk to Seek Permission

Because if we had just one hour in your sun
We'd show you how it's done
We'd show you how quickly things can turn around
Go on, give us one hour in your sun
And watch us bloom a field of colour
Look, look how our labours blossom
Look how we flourish with no sun, no heat or warmth
Because we know how to make love grow in the frost
In the hard dirt, in the winter underground
We make magic mushrooms from shit
And spin gold from flakes of hard life
Our hunger is bears, our thirst we share
No boots, no armour, nothing but love drives this
And love is where this comes from and
Love is who this is for and love knows
We have nothing but each other to protect this
No gloves, bare hands, no certainties
And no money, no, never any money
So go on, I dare you, and I dare it
Give us a go on your sun and watch how we'd share it
Give us a paddle in your sunlight, a splash of shiny-shiny
One hour of the sun that is fixed on you and your privilege
For look how strong we are and how tall we can already stand
Without your sun, without your gold and
Without your permission.

Sage

The hot moon
has nudged us awake
called us come
bare foot
naked hearted
stones circle the flame

we cut and burn a ringlet
for all the memory hair holds
of you and of then

slit a fish throat
metaphorically
open the sea
and all the wet sky
and then let go
of all those gulped words

it's safe to cough them up now
your throat jammed with rage
and furry with unspoken things

remember how they shushed you
for you were being a girl
too loud they said
and such messy hair

then when you grew
beautiful and strong
you were still all wrong
so laugh, belly laugh

your teeth all liquorice
your face is a festival
mud and ash
smoke and cider

daub their doll's house in clots
add salt for the truth of it
and pepper for the courage this always takes
every lifetime over and over again

you are the survivor
of ideas that cannot burn
you are your own
ghost's wildest dream

here's some sage
stick that in your
bowl and smoke it

burn ear wax
for all the listening
they will not do
an eyelash
for the lucky charms of you

prick your finger
and write in blood:
I promise I will never ever shush

then roar
bold enough to wake your elders
pour oil on the fire
and spit and crackle
as all your hurts uncurl

add water
she remembers everyone
every drop of every one of us
be seen for which drop you are
the truth of it shines in your tears

take a good slug of rum
and then swig another
and feel the burn
look it in the terrible eye
the spirit walking in your veins

you won't bleed
for much longer
the trouble of it leaves you

tie it with string
place them feelings
in the doll's house
lock it, nice and neat
and miniature

and watch it burn
hot and orange and true
you'll never shush or shrink

finish the bottle of rum
leave none for the dying stars
nothing for the postman

bloody moon
midsummer's furious beauty
in a world that never changes
so march forwards

I promise
I will never ever shush you
we hold hands
love shines brightest
just then as the moon sets
since all this blood began
we never, ever

give up.

While Justice Waits

there they go again
filling your mouth
with their name

there they go again
adding more weight
to your burden

there they go again
giving you all this anxiety
whilst telling you not to panic
when the panic is rooted in
centuries of ...
there they go again
there they go again

there they go again
contradicting their own rules
double speak and double standards

there they go again
your dead are statistics
your ghosts live in hashtags

there they go again
getting away with murder
but calling it anything else

there they go again
doing nothing as your vulnerable
and sick and dying
need all your love and care
and your living need all of your
focus, energy and time

there they go again
filling your plate
with their jobs
and the work
they should do
as your elected leaders

there they go again,
dominating your thoughts
so no work can get done

there they go again
grimacing on the front page
hogging the limelight
with performative cruelty

there they go again
suffocating light and hope
like a pillow held fast over the face
of the kicking and struggling truth

there they go again
consuming all the oxygen
and rewriting history

there they go again
like it's all about them
but it is because of them
and it is in spite of them

there they go again
obscuring the facts
blurring the edges
blinkering the horse
filtering the picture

there they go again
there they go again
there they go again

and it is not the names of the dead
nor the name of the nurse
not the name of the innocent
but their name in your mouth

how can it be?
that when you wake in the night
wailing and mourning and hurting
they are marching on your tongue
they are renting your insomnia

there they go again
using your anguish as garnish
using your defence as an attack
using your fear to divide you
using your rage to pass draconian laws
using your pain to sell shit back to you
using your grief to decorate newspapers
using your anger to kill you

because there they go again
there they go again
there they go again
casting an ass in the lead role
the wealthy politicians in the spotlight
the hideous clown gets top billing
the monster as the headline act

your horror gets a walk on part
your mourning cries are extras
your fury is the chorus line
your humanity the supporting cast

while justice waits in the wings

Before You Go

Before you go to the doctors
and take their anti-depressants
before you numb yourself with gin
and before you sign up for a shrink
and yet more counselling
to cope with your escalating
anxiety and panic attacks,

Before you go and give
yourself another scolding
for feeling overtired
for cancelling things
for feeling hypersensitive
for not going faster
for being too slow
for not being stronger and
for not being more decisive,

Please check you are not in fact in mourning
and living in a world ruled by rude twats,
impatient and selfish arseholes
in a careless, noisy, and filthy world,
governed by the corruption of reckless criminals
that should listen to the nightmares of children.

Every Disaster Movie Begins with the Government Ignoring a Scientist

Every
disaster movie
begins with
the government
ignoring the signs—
the barking dog
the flight of birds
the stomach contents
of a dead whale
the rising temperature
the colour of the rainwater
a worried mother
an enlightened being
the poet, the artist
the prophecy
the writing on the wall
the lyrics of songs
the child's nightmares
the poor and the sick
every disaster film
has everyone
ignoring
the people
begging
for change.

Tomorrow's Roses

I ask for tomorrow's roses
not a bunch from the garage
not a steal from the park
not a luxury bouquet
no fancy garnish and bows

but tomorrow's roses
their roots in mud in our yard
growing stronger every day
with the promise of sun
and light and warmth

that you will be here with me
to see all tomorrow's roses grow
means everything and more
that you will be here with me
to share the summer and the flowers

that you will be there in our backyard
watching the sun setting
green parakeets fly overhead
the sky all soft and pink above
as we share a cold evening beer
and water the tomatoes

our promises all blooming
a rose as big as my face
so glorious and sweet
that colour and that feeling
of you and me holding hands
when tomorrow comes.

Pessimism is for Lightweights

Think of those that marched this road before
And those that will march here in years to come
The road in shadow and the road in the sun
The road before us and the road all done
History is watching us and what will we become

This road is all flags and milestones
Immigrant blood and sweat and tears
Built this city, built this country
Made this road last all these years

This road is made of protest
And those not permitted to vote
And those that are still fighting to speak
With a boot stamping on their throat

There is power and strength in optimism
To have faith and to stay true to you
Because if you can look in the mirror
And have belief and promise you
Will share wonder in living things
Beauty, dreams, books and art
Love your neighbour and be kind
And have an open heart

Then you're already winning at living
You speak up, you show up and stand tall
It's silence that is complicit
It's apathy that hurts us all

Pessimism is for lightweights
This road was never easy or straight
And living is all about living alive and lively
And I believe love will conquer hate.

Orwenness biþ for Leohtwyhtum
translation by Emily Cotman

Aman þam þæt foron þas stræte ær
Ond þam þæt faraþ toweardum gearum
Stræte sceaduwe ond stræte sunnan
Stræte us beforan ond stræte ærgedon
Gerecedness[1] us wæcceþ—hwæt sculen we weorðan

Þeos stræt biþ eall fana ond mearca
Friþbena[2] blod ond swat ond tearas
Byldon þas burg, byldon þis land
Macodon stræte biran ealle þas gear

Þeos stræt biþ of wiðre
Ond þæm naaþ to ceosan
Ond þæm þæt giet sæcaþ asprecan
Amang scoh stempþ on hira[3] ceolan

Þær biþ eafoð ond rice of hyhtfulnesse[4]
Habban geleafan ond beon þin sylf þu[5]
For gif meaht þu aseon þin licnesse[6]
Ond habban treowe ond geæðan þu
Scealt gædere awundran in cwice þinge
Glæm, cræft, bec ond swefn
Lufian neahgeburas[7] ond beon glæd
Ond habban gerumene sefan[8]

Þan þu giet spedest æt lif
Þu æfnest, acweðest, ond standest deall[9]
Hit biþ salnes[10] þæt biþ scyldig[11]
Caldheortnes[12] þæt hearmaþ eall

Orwenness biþ for leohtwyhtum[13]
Þeos stræt wære næfre rihte ond eaþe
Ond libban biþ eall ymb libban liffæst ond liflic[14]
Ond gelyfe ic ðæt lufu abriceþ hete

Pessimism is for Lightweights

reverse translation

Think of those that traveled this road before
And those that travel in future years
Road in shadow and road in sun
Road before us and road done before
History watches us—what shall we become

This road is all flags and milestones
Refugee blood and sweat and tears
Built this city, built this nation
Made road endure all these years

This road is of resistance
And those not permitted to choose
And those that still fight to speak
While a shoe stamps on their throat

There is strength and power in hopefulness
To have faith and be you yourself
For if you can look at your likeness
And have trust and swear you
Shall together wonder at living things
Beauty, art, books and dreams
Love neighbours and be kind
And have an open heart

Then you already succeed at life
You show up, speak, and stand proud
It is silence that is guilty
Cold-heartedness that harms all

Pessimism is for lightweights
This road was never straight and easy
And to live is all about living alive and life-giving
And I believe that love conquers hate

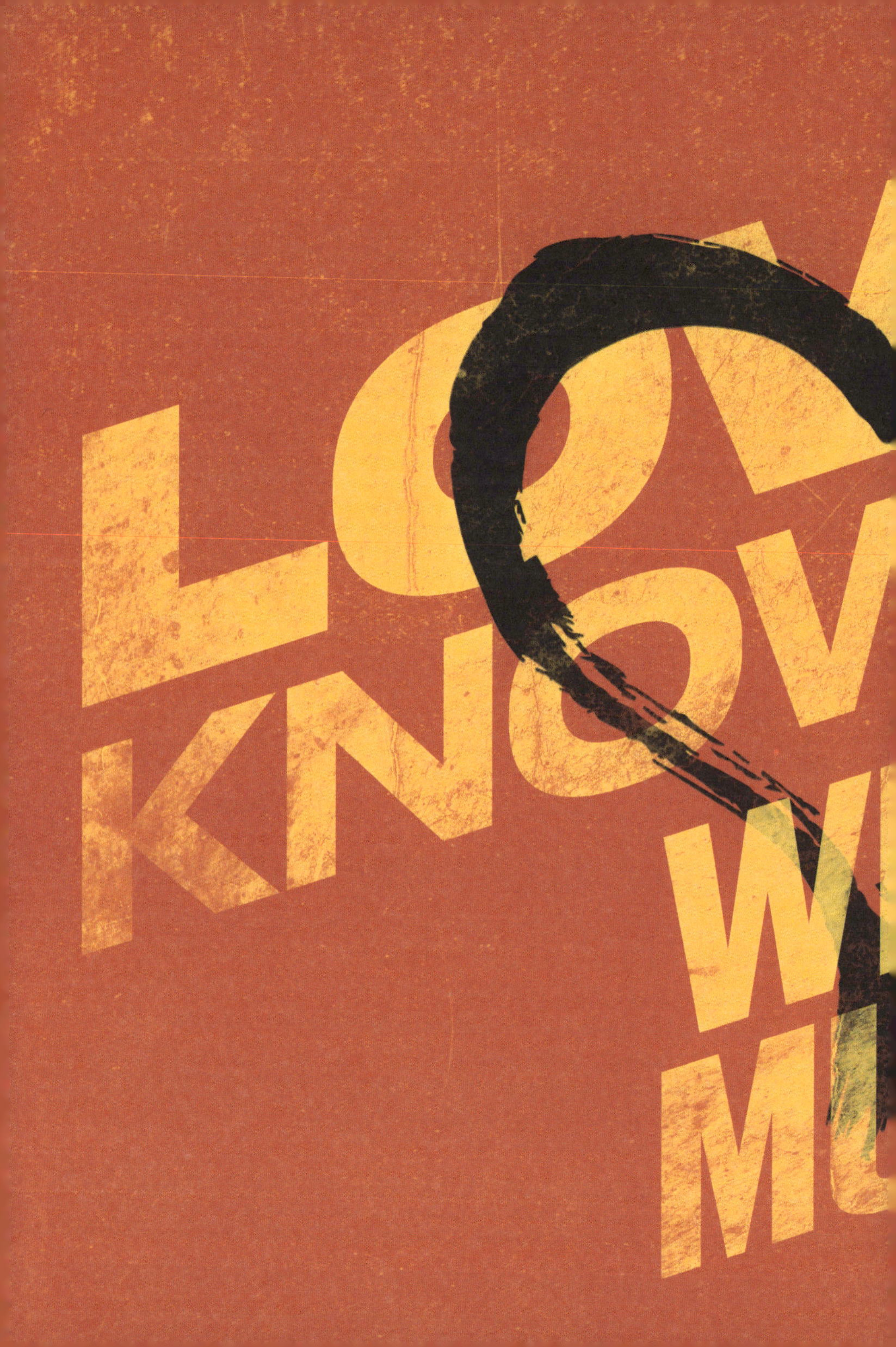
LO
KNO
W
M

'S
HAVE SO
CH TO DO

Notes

1 Historical notions of history are... slippery. In modern times, we use the word 'history' with an assumed objectivity. But we know that depending on who is holding the pen, the facts of history vary wildly. So when it comes to the word for 'history' in Old English, well... Are we talking about the history of saints and martyrs? The ecclesiastical calendar? The Gordian-Knot tales of devils, gods, and kings? OE *gerecedness* refers to a narrative of events, an interpretation or retelling of them, which seems fitting here. It also sounds like 'wretchedness,' and honestly, I love that for us.

2 Given the state of the world for which Godden wrote this poem, I'm fairly certain these 'immigrants' aren't American ex-pats, comfortably retired. There are words in OE for 'travelers', 'pilgrims', and 'exiles', but in this context, 'refugees' seems most appropriate. Hence, the gorgeous Old English word *friþbena*, which translates literally to 'peace-petitioner'.

3 Since 'throat' is singular, I read this as a singular 'their'. I'm not sure if speakers of OE used a singular 'they/their/theirs,' but they should have. Chaucer did, which is only about 400 years' difference, and what's 400 years compared to the age of Watling Street? Nothin' is what. Let's hold space here and now for the queer kids in the tenth century. *We eow geseoþ, leoflicu.*

4 This poem references a handful of philosophical concepts for which no direct translations are available. 'Optimism', 'pessimism', etc. are storage crates built by Voltaire and Friends during the 17th-18th centuries to contain select elements of the human experience. People in the tenth century felt these things, even if we don't see them called out in the corpus. Anyway, I've translated 'optimism' here as *hyhtfulness*, meaning 'the state of being full of hope', because to me, real optimism is something like 'hope, with claws'.

5 Old English boasts a variety of 'you's. I chose the singular *þu* for this and the next few stanzas, to honor the signature intimacy of Godden's work. Whether she's addressing a crowd of thousands or a single radio host, listening to the poet read and sing feels as though we're old friends sitting together over a coffee.

6 I took some artistic liberties here, since there isn't a great OE word for 'mirror' (there simply weren't many around). What seems important about this moment is not the object itself, but the action of facing oneself as another might. Hence the substitution, *licness* ('likeness').

7 I have nothing insightful to say about this word... I'm just absolutely jazzed to learn that it's so old.

8 Can you believe that *swefn/sefan* works as an end-rhyme? Astonishing! Usually OE is a righteous pain in the ass about rhyming, soit feels all the sweeter when it cooperates.

9 'Tall' became 'proud' for the sake of the rhyme. For the sake of the art.

10 Many, many thanks to Salena Godden for the opportunity—and I am not being sarcastic—to read K. Haughland's dissertation on the History of the Cleft Sentence Structure in the English Language. Keep your blockbusters—it's the evolution of syntactic abstraction that thrills me.

11 'Complicit' is another word we adopted from the French around the 17th century—too young for a direct translation. So, I went bold—'complicit' simply became 'guilty' (*scyldig*), which shifts the harm caused by silence from an association to an ownership.

12 What makes apathy so dangerous to a community—more than disinterest or idleness—is that a truly apathetic personcan't be emotionally moved. Many white people (like myself) admit to feeling 'frozen' with respect to racial justice action. This inspired my choice of cold-heartedness (*caldheortness*), which undeniably 'hurts us all'.

13 This phrase was naturally the first thing I translated. Finding something suitable encouraged me to keep going. For 'pessimism', I chose *orwenness*, meaning 'hopelessness, despair'. The unethical thing about harboring pessimism is not that you bring the room down, but that you've given up, called it a loss, and left a mess for others to clean. For 'lightweights', I constructed a compound word which I'm certain must have existed already. The two halves of the word translated recognizably as *leoht* and *gewiht*. OE *leoht* carried figurative meanings as well as the literal 'un-heavy'. These included 'fickle', 'easy', and 'negligible'. *Gewyht* meant 'weight' and could be shortened to *-wyht* when used in compound words. *Wiht* also meant 'creature, being'. So we end up with a nice homonym—*leohtwyht*, meaning both 'lightweight' and 'fickle creature'.

14 I chose to preserve the consonance in this line at the expense of some semantic nuance. (e.g. OE *liffæst* is rather clinical, compared with Modern 'alive'). I just couldn't bear to lose the playful pivoting around the root word 'life'. Sometimes the harmony between words communicates more than any one word's definition, which seems to be the case here.

Definitions from the Bosworth-Toller Anglo-Saxon Dictionary

ACKNOWLEDGEMENTS

I first heard the phrase *Pessimism is for Lightweights* in a talk John Higgs gave at Daisy Campbell's *Cosmic Trigger* play. Huge thank you to John Higgs who commissioned me to write this poem for the *Watling Street* book and podcast and thank you also for your generous foreword to this edition of these poems. In 2018, this poem was on display at the Arnolfini Gallery, Bristol, with thanks to gallery director Claire Doherty. Since then, this poem has been donated to the People's History Museum in Manchester where it is now on permanent display.

Courage is a Muscle was written for the Women's March and performed at Downing Street in January 2018. *The Day We Stopped* was a commission written for Festival of the Future City 2017. Exploring migration, *The Letter* was commissioned in collaboration with Jerwood Composer Jasmin Kent Rodgman, for performance with the London Symphony Orchestra at LSO St Luke's, London in March 2018. *Soup* was broadcast several times on the BBC and has also been published, with thanks to Tim Wells, in Rising Zine and The New River Press.

In September 2017 I made *Red* into a poem-film with Richard Cripps and lots of jam and fake blood, and we donated it to *Nasty Women*, a London art show that raised money to combat violence against women and girls and a global art movement that serves to demonstrate solidarity in the face of threats to roll back women's rights, individual rights, and abortion rights. More recently the poem *Red* was included in *The Most Powerful Woman in the Universe* exhibition, a feminist group show curated by painter Kelly-Anne Davitt at Gallery 46, Whitechapel, London in September 2019. Following on from this, parts of this poem have been updated and translated into Polish and published in POETIKI anthology in 2021 with thanks to Bartosz Wójcik. *I Saw Goody Proctor Jogging Without a Face Mask* has also been translated and published in Poland with thanks again to Bartosz Wójcik.

Welcome to Hope was written in lockdown and donated to the Charleston Trust and featured on BBC Radio 2 for National Poetry Day. *Pink Moon* was a commission by The Verb on BBC Radio 3 in 2020. Music to this mirror poem has been composed and performed by Anna Phoebe. Our lockdown collaborations were performed and filmed remotely and shared at York Cathedral, York Festival. *Not Every Thing is True* was published in *The Dizziness Of Freedom* anthology by Bad Betty Press. *Chapter* and *Tomorrow's Roses* were published in Platypus Press. *No Holds Barred* was published by Tangerine Press as part of their Underground Poems series. *While Justice Waits* was written for the Black Lives Matter movement. It was an honour to perform this piece for the first time live on stage at Rich Mix for Black Lives Matter founder Patrisse Cullors as part of her OWN IT! London book tour in spring 2022. Lastly, three poems, *While Justice Waits, Chapter* and *Who is Us, Who is Them* are published in a special edition of Wasafari commissioned by guest editor Darren Chetty.

Thank you to Nina Hervé, Will Burns, Craig Oldham and the Rough Trade Books family. Thanks to Canongate Books and OWN IT! Thanks to Matt Abbott and Nymphs and Thugs. Thank you for all of your support. Special thank you to Dickie for all tomorrow's roses, for always and for everything.

Salena Godden FRSL is an award-winning author, poet and broadcaster of Jamaican-mixed heritage. Her work has been widely anthologised and broadcast on radio, TV and film. She regularly headlines international literary festivals and has published several titles: *Under The Pier, Fishing In The Aftermath, Springfield Road* and *Pessimism is for Lightweights—13 Pieces of Courage and Resistance*. Her poem "Pessimism is for Lightweights" is on permanent display at People's History Museum, Manchester. Godden's debut novel *Mrs Death Misses Death* (Canongate) won the Indie Book Award for Fiction and the People's Book Prize 2022 and was shortlisted for a British Book Award and the Gordon Burn Prize. Film and TV rights for *Mrs Death Misses Death* have been optioned by Idris Elba's production company Green Door Pictures. Godden is currently working on three new books out soon with Canongate: a memoir, a poetry collection and an eagerly anticipated second novel set in the *Mrs Death Misses Death* universe. Godden was inducted as a fellow of The Royal Society of Literature in 2022.

www.salenagodden.co.uk

Emily Cotman (they/she) writes in the margins of the work week and dabbles in reanimating the dead. Their words appear in Lumpen Journal, The Madrigal, Stone Canoe & elsewhere. They live gratefully on Gayogohó:no' land.